U.S.A. TRAVEL GUIDES

SOUTH CAROLINA

BY ANN HEINRICHS • ILLUSTRATED BY MATT KANIA

The
Child's
World®
childsworld.com

Published by The Child's World®
1980 Lookout Drive • Mankato, MN 56003-1705
800-599-READ • www.childsworld.com

ISBN 9781503819801
LCCN 2016961624

Printing
Printed in the United States of America
PA02334

Ann Heinrichs is the author of more than 100 books for children and young adults. She has also enjoyed successful careers as a children's book editor and an advertising copywriter. Ann grew up in Fort Smith, Arkansas, and lives in Chicago, Illinois.

post card

About the Author
Ann Heinrichs

Matt Kania loves maps and, as a kid, dreamed of making them. In school he studied geography and cartography, and today he makes maps for a living. Matt's favorite thing about drawing maps is learning about the places they represent. Many of the maps he has created can be found in books, magazines, videos, Web sites, and public places.

post card

About the
Map Illustrator
Matt Kania

On the cover: Visit the many attractions at Myrtle Beach.

OUR SOUTH CAROLINA TRIP

SOUTH CAROLINA

Ready to explore the Palmetto State? Then hop aboard. We're heading for South Carolina! Just follow that loopy dotted line. Or else skip around. Either way, you're in for a great adventure.

You'll meet tree frogs, sea turtles, and otters. You'll see sand dunes and waterfalls. You'll learn about battles that shaped the nation. You'll eat chitlins and grits. And you'll visit two very different factories. One makes cars. The other is a goat farm! Are you curious? Then buckle up and hang on tight. We're off!

WELCOME TO
SOUTH CAROLINA

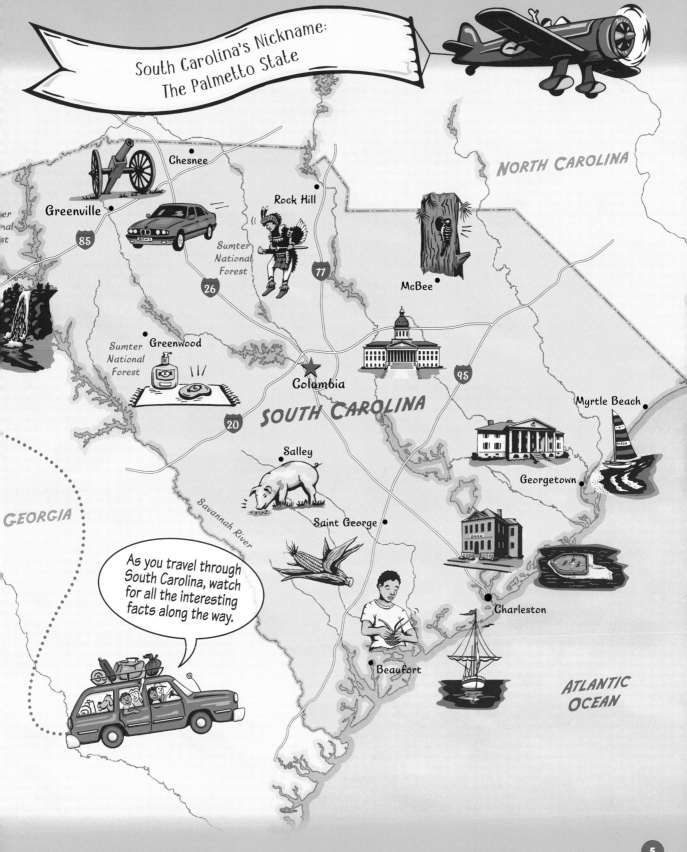

South Carolina's Nickname:
The Palmetto State

NORTH CAROLINA

Chesnee

Greenville

Rock Hill

McBee

Sumter National Forest

Greenwood

Sumter National Forest

Columbia

SOUTH CAROLINA

Myrtle Beach

Salley

Georgetown

Savannah River

Saint George

GEORGIA

Charleston

As you travel through South Carolina, watch for all the interesting facts along the way.

Beaufort

ATLANTIC OCEAN

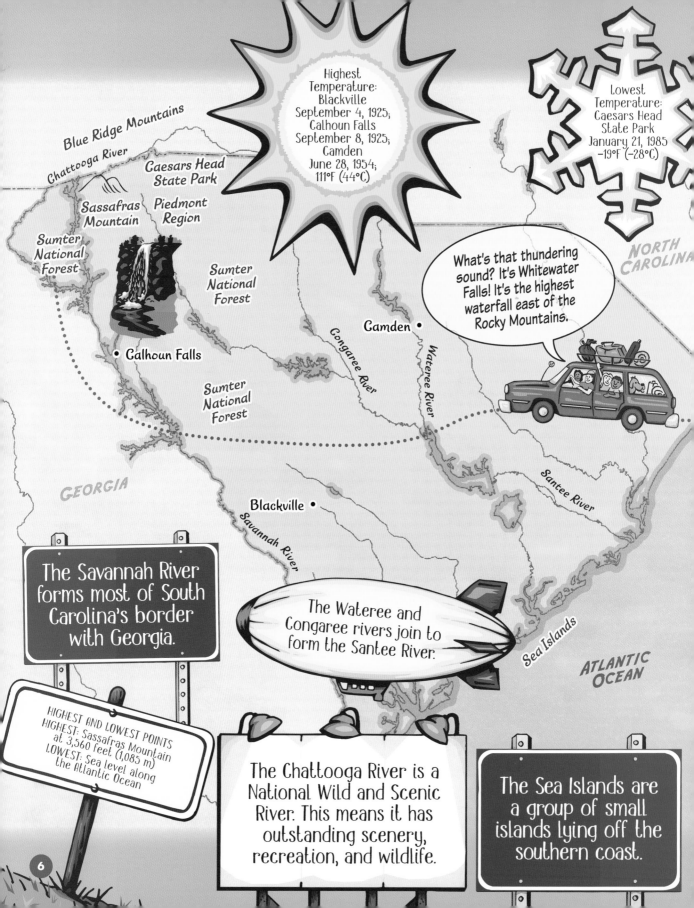

Blue Ridge Mountains

Chattooga River

Caesars Head State Park

Sassafras Mountain

Piedmont Region

Sumter National Forest

Sumter National Forest

Sumter National Forest

• Calhoun Falls

Highest Temperature: Blackville September 4, 1925; Calhoun Falls September 8, 1925; Camden June 28, 1954; 111°F (44°C)

Lowest Temperature: Caesars Head State Park January 21, 1985 –19°F (–28°C)

NORTH CAROLINA

Camden •

Congaree River

Wateree River

What's that thundering sound? It's Whitewater Falls! It's the highest waterfall east of the Rocky Mountains.

GEORGIA

Blackville •

Savannah River

Santee River

Sea Islands

ATLANTIC OCEAN

The Savannah River forms most of South Carolina's border with Georgia.

The Wateree and Congaree rivers join to form the Santee River.

HIGHEST AND LOWEST POINTS
HIGHEST: Sassafras Mountain at 3,560 feet (1,085 m)
LOWEST: Sea level along the Atlantic Ocean

The Chattooga River is a National Wild and Scenic River. This means it has outstanding scenery, recreation, and wildlife.

The Sea Islands are a group of small islands lying off the southern coast.

6

SUMTER NATIONAL FOREST IN THE BLUE RIDGE REGION

Paddle your canoe down the Chattooga River. It twists and turns through the forest. Or take a hiking trail. You'll pass beautiful waterfalls.

You're enjoying Sumter National Forest. The forest is in three different parts in South Carolina's northwest corner. The Blue Ridge Mountains run through this area. The hilly Piedmont Region slopes down from there. South Carolina's hilly regions are called the upcountry.

The lowcountry is the state's largest region. It's a wide coastal plain. Southeastern South Carolina faces the Atlantic Ocean. Many areas near the coast are **swamps**.

The Chattooga River Trail is more than 40 miles (64 km) long.

Admire the sand dunes. Gather some seashells. Catch a fish. Or maybe you like noisy fun. Then hop on a ride at the amusement park. You can do it all at Myrtle Beach!

Many popular beaches line South Carolina's coast. Myrtle Beach is on the northeast coast. Hilton Head Island is a favorite spot, too. It's just off the southeast coast.

South Carolina is also a great place for racing. Camden holds the Carolina Cup horse race. Darlington is known for its car races. And there are sailboat races off the coast.

Stay all day and watch the sun set at Myrtle Beach.

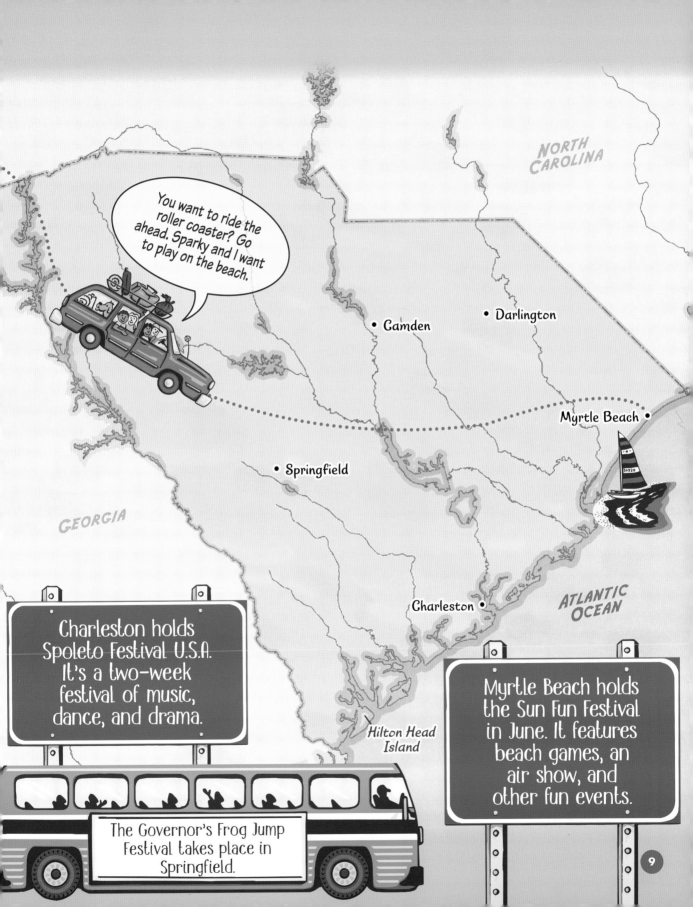

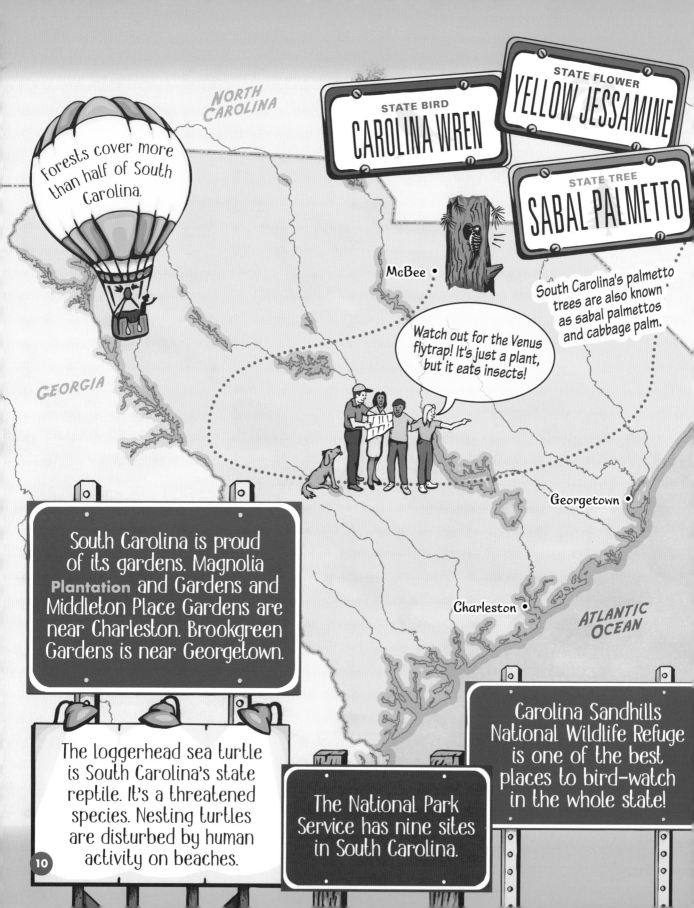

NORTH CAROLINA

Forests cover more than half of South Carolina.

STATE BIRD
CAROLINA WREN

STATE FLOWER
YELLOW JESSAMINE

STATE TREE
SABAL PALMETTO

McBee •

South Carolina's palmetto trees are also known as sabal palmettos and cabbage palm.

Watch out for the Venus flytrap! It's just a plant, but it eats insects!

GEORGIA

Georgetown •

South Carolina is proud of its gardens. Magnolia **Plantation** and Gardens and Middleton Place Gardens are near Charleston. Brookgreen Gardens is near Georgetown.

Charleston •

ATLANTIC OCEAN

The loggerhead sea turtle is South Carolina's state reptile. It's a threatened species. Nesting turtles are disturbed by human activity on beaches.

The National Park Service has nine sites in South Carolina.

Carolina Sandhills National Wildlife Refuge is one of the best places to bird-watch in the whole state!

CAROLINA SANDHILLS NATIONAL WILDLIFE REFUGE NEAR McBEE

You'll love exploring Carolina Sandhills National Wildlife Refuge. There's so much going on!

Do you hear a chirping sound? It's a little green tree frog. You may see fox squirrels on the ground. People sometimes mistake them for foxes!

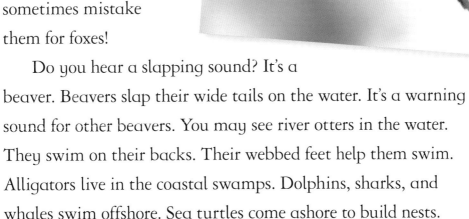

Do you hear a slapping sound? It's a beaver. Beavers slap their wide tails on the water. It's a warning sound for other beavers. You may see river otters in the water. They swim on their backs. Their webbed feet help them swim. Alligators live in the coastal swamps. Dolphins, sharks, and whales swim offshore. Sea turtles come ashore to build nests.

The refuge is home to many animals but mostly focuses on preserving the life of the red-cockaded woodpecker.

THE DAY OF THE CATAWBA AT ROCK HILL

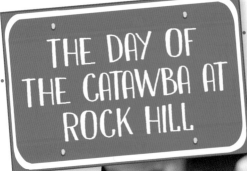

The dancers all wear **traditional** dress. Feathers and fringe swirl with each movement. These Native American performers are Catawba people. They're celebrating Yap Ye Iswa. That means "Day of the Catawba."

Thousands of Native Americans lived in the area now known as South Carolina for centuries before Europeans arrived. The Catawba knew which plants to use as medicine. They passed on their history through storytelling.

Spanish explorers arrived in the 1500s. Spaniards tried to establish a **colony** in 1526. They left after a few months, though. French **colonists** came in 1562. They soon left, too. Spaniards returned in 1566. They established Santa Elena on Parris Island.

A Catawba man performs a dance wearing traditional clothing.

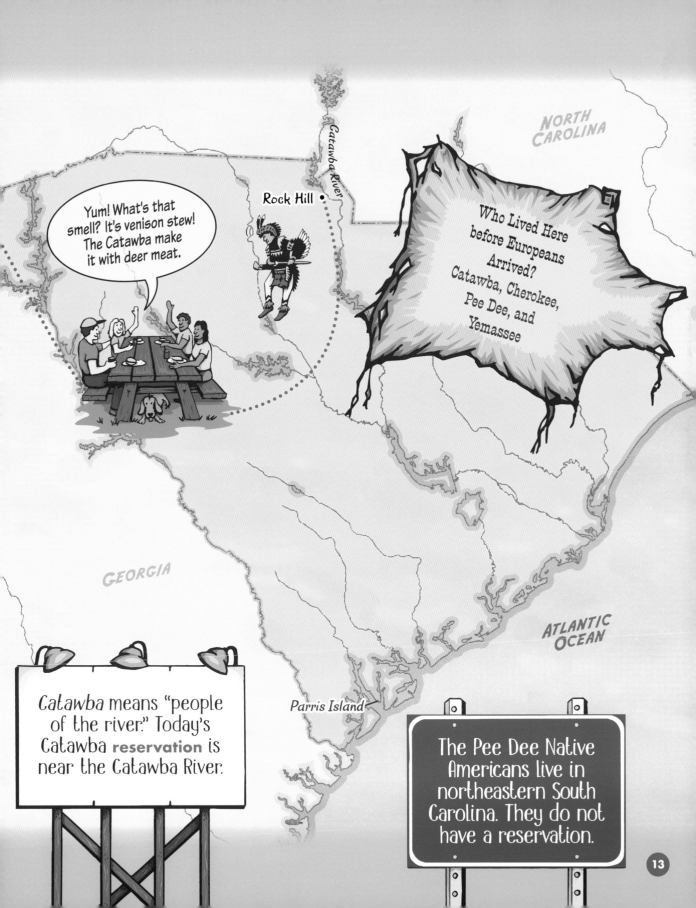

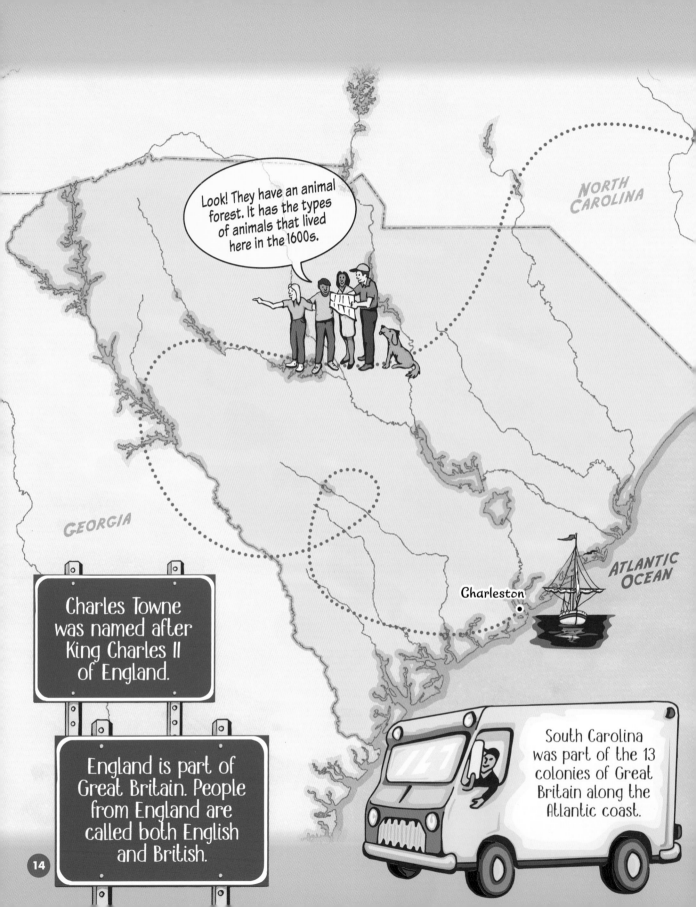

CHARLES TOWNE LANDING

Climb aboard the *Adventure*. It's built just like the colonists' trading ships. Then stroll through the village. It's just like a colonial town in the 1600s.

You're exploring Charles Towne Landing. English colonists settled here in 1670. In 1680, they moved to Oyster Point. This became Charleston, South Carolina's first permanent town.

South Carolina's early settlers lived near the coast. Many of them grew rice. They sent their products out on ships. Charleston grew to be a busy port city.

A group of English noblemen set up the Carolina Colony. The colony split in 1729. It became North Carolina and South Carolina.

The Adventure *isn't the real ship. It's a replica, or copy, of what ships would have looked like in the 1600s.*

Would you like to step back 300 years? That's easy. Just visit Charleston's historic district. It preserves many buildings from Charleston's early days.

Charleston was a wealthy city in the 1700s. Ships sailed in and out of its port. The Exchange and Provost Building still stands today. Merchants handled their shipping business there.

Some ships brought in people from Africa. They were sold in the marketplace as slaves. You can still see the Old Slave Mart. Another historic building is Market Hall and Sheds. People sold fresh vegetables and meat there.

Take a tour of downtown Charleston in a horse carriage.

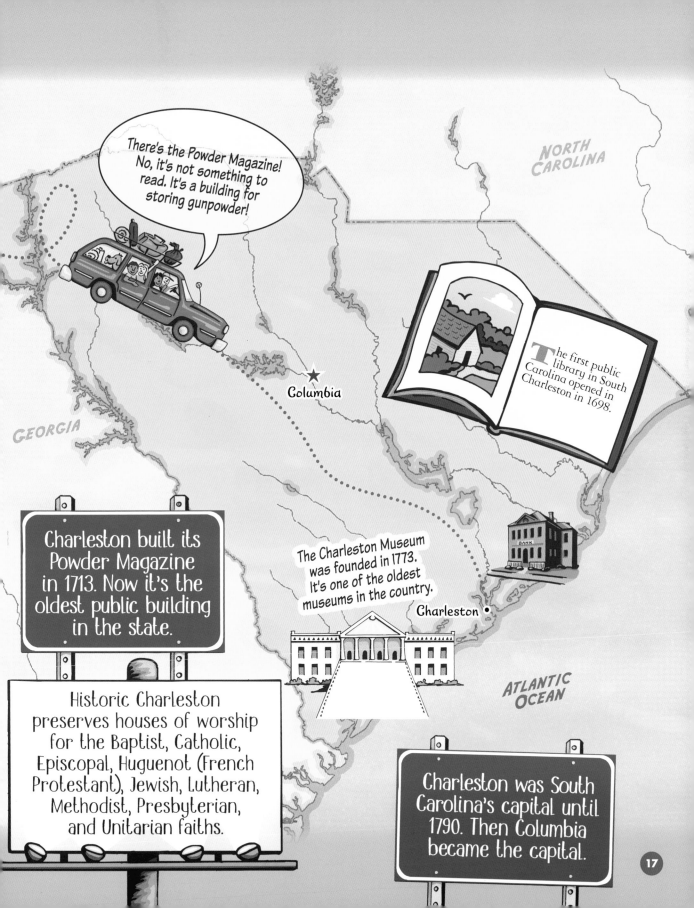

There's the Powder Magazine! No, it's not something to read. It's a building for storing gunpowder!

The first public library in South Carolina opened in Charleston in 1698.

NORTH CAROLINA

★ Columbia

GEORGIA

Charleston built its Powder Magazine in 1713. Now it's the oldest public building in the state.

The Charleston Museum was founded in 1773. It's one of the oldest museums in the country.

Charleston

Historic Charleston preserves houses of worship for the Baptist, Catholic, Episcopal, Huguenot (French Protestant), Jewish, Lutheran, Methodist, Presbyterian, and Unitarian faiths.

ATLANTIC OCEAN

Charleston was South Carolina's capital until 1790. Then Columbia became the capital.

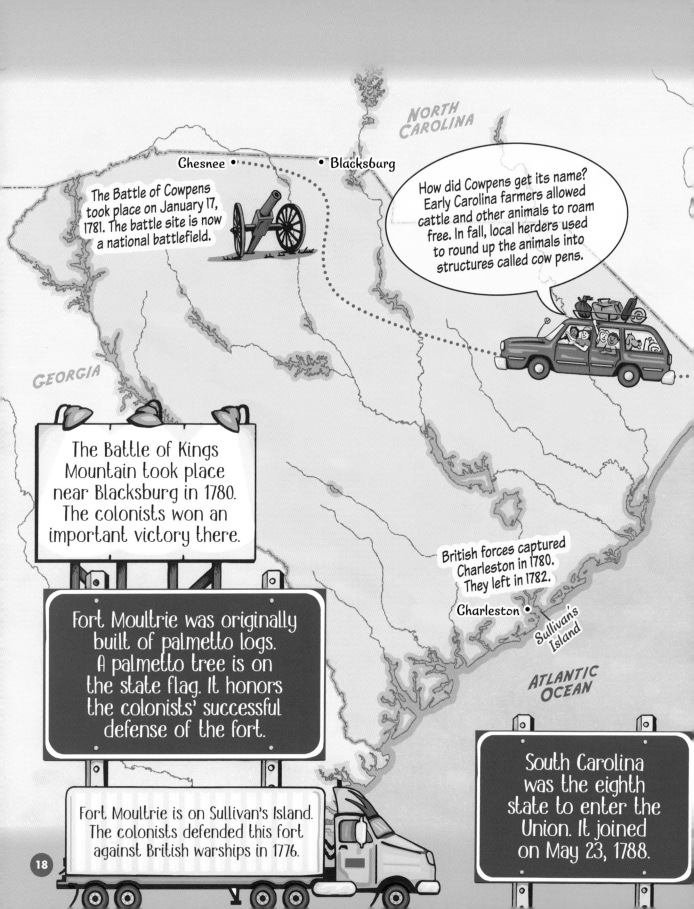

NORTH CAROLINA

Chesnee • Blacksburg

The Battle of Cowpens took place on January 17, 1781. The battle site is now a national battlefield.

How did Cowpens get its name? Early Carolina farmers allowed cattle and other animals to roam free. In fall, local herders used to round up the animals into structures called cow pens.

GEORGIA

The Battle of Kings Mountain took place near Blacksburg in 1780. The colonists won an important victory there.

British forces captured Charleston in 1780. They left in 1782.

Charleston •

Sullivan's Island

Fort Moultrie was originally built of palmetto logs. A palmetto tree is on the state flag. It honors the colonists' successful defense of the fort.

ATLANTIC OCEAN

Fort Moultrie is on Sullivan's Island. The colonists defended this fort against British warships in 1776.

South Carolina was the eighth state to enter the Union. It joined on May 23, 1788.

COWPENS NATIONAL BATTLEFIELD NEAR CHESNEE

In time, the colonists wanted their freedom. They fought Great Britain in the Revolutionary War (1775–1783).

Colonial troops won some big victories in South Carolina. One victory was at the Battle of Cowpens. You can visit the battlefield today. Exhibits at the visitors' center explain what happened.

Special events take place on the battle's anniversary. People dress like Revolutionary War soldiers. They show how the colonists fired their guns.

The war was hard, but the colonists were tough. They won! The colonies became the United States of America.

Actors often reenact the Battle of Cowpens.

Wander through the elegant **mansion**. Stroll through the fields. Things are quiet at Hampton Plantation now. But it was once bustling with activity.

Hampton Plantation grew rice. That was South Carolina's leading crop in the 1700s. Coastal farmers still raised rice into the 1800s. By the mid-1800s, cotton was the major crop. Enslaved African Americans worked on the plantations.

Northern and Southern states argued about slavery. Most Southerners were in favor of slavery. But many Northerners were against it. This conflict grew into the Civil War (1861–1865).

The Hampton Plantation has a lot of history. Take a tour to learn all about it!

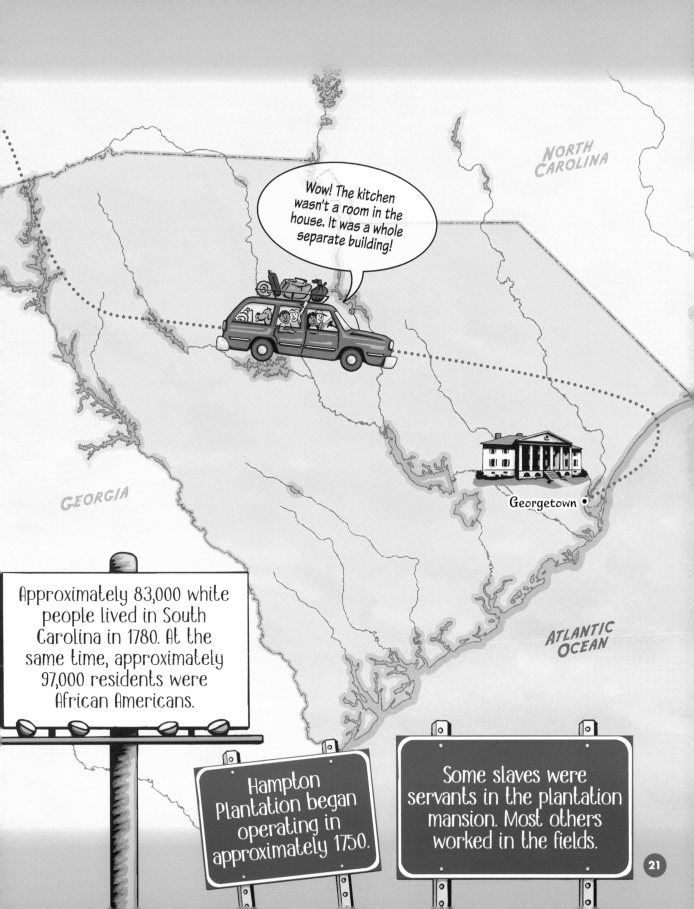

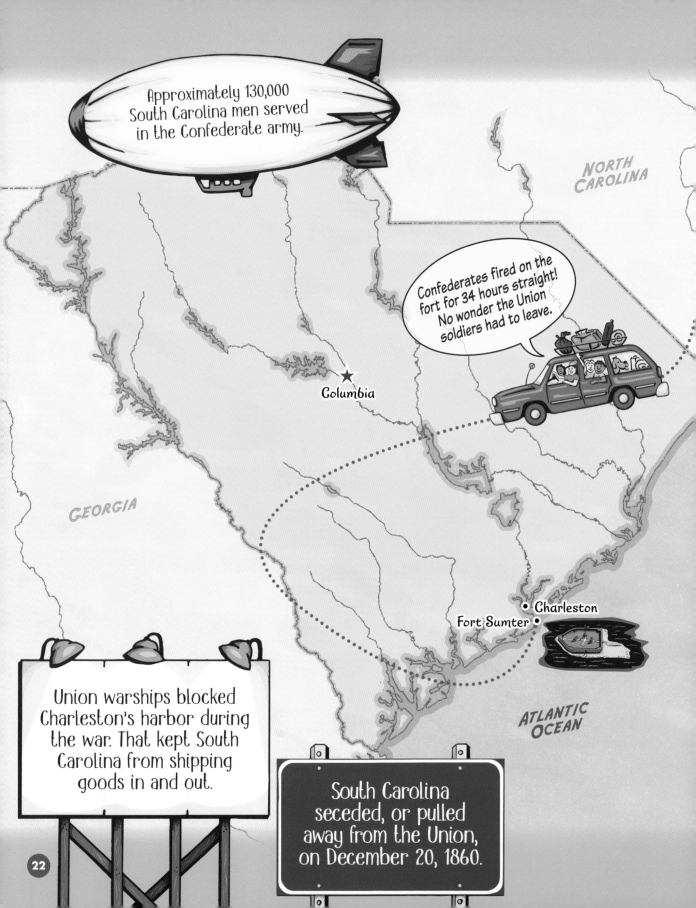

Approximately 130,000 South Carolina men served in the Confederate army.

Confederates fired on the fort for 34 hours straight! No wonder the Union soldiers had to leave.

NORTH CAROLINA

★ Columbia

GEORGIA

• Charleston
Fort Sumter •

ATLANTIC OCEAN

Union warships blocked Charleston's harbor during the war. That kept South Carolina from shipping goods in and out.

South Carolina seceded, or pulled away from the Union, on December 20, 1860.

Cannons still stand around Fort Sumter. You reach this island fort by boat.

Slavery was a growing issue among the states. Southern states, such as South Carolina, thought slavery should be allowed. Northern states did not. Then South Carolina pulled away from the Union. Other Southern states followed. They formed the Confederate States of America.

U.S. troops occupied Fort Sumter. On April 12, 1861, Confederates fired on the fort. Union troops were forced to surrender. That began the Civil War.

Union general William Tecumseh Sherman marched through South Carolina. His soldiers burned Columbia and many plantations. In the end, the Union won the war.

Fort Sumter was built in 1829 and still stands today.

THE STATE CAPITOL IN COLUMBIA

Stroll around the outside of the capitol. Keep your eyes on the wall. Here and there, you'll see metal stars. They're a reminder of Civil War days. In 1865, Union soldiers fired cannons on the capitol. The stars mark the spots where cannonballs struck.

Inside the capitol are state government offices. South Carolina's government is divided into three branches. One branch makes the state's laws. Another branch carries out those laws. It's headed by the governor. The third branch is made up of judges. They decide whether someone has broken the law.

Take a look at the place where South Carolina laws are made.

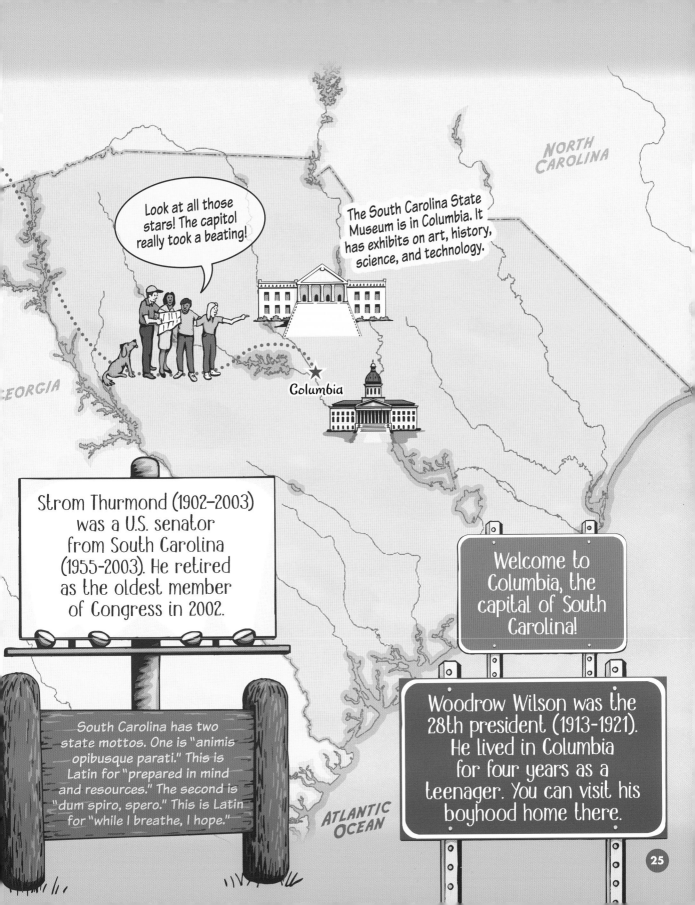

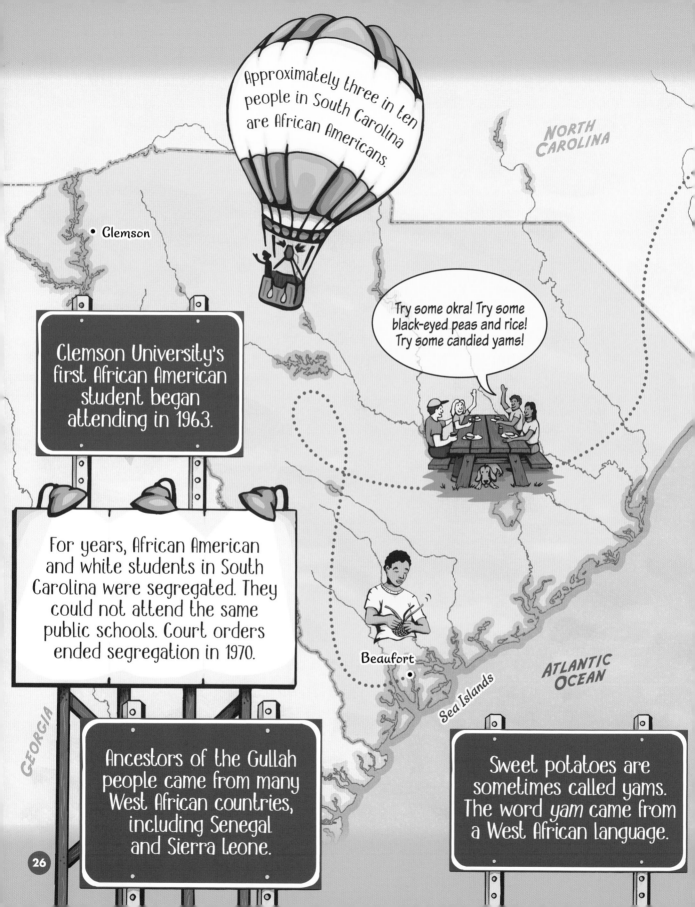

Approximately three in ten people in South Carolina are African Americans.

• Clemson

NORTH CAROLINA

Clemson University's first African American student began attending in 1963.

Try some okra! Try some black-eyed peas and rice! Try some candied yams!

For years, African American and white students in South Carolina were segregated. They could not attend the same public schools. Court orders ended segregation in 1970.

Beaufort

ATLANTIC OCEAN

GEORGIA

Sea Islands

Ancestors of the Gullah people came from many West African countries, including Senegal and Sierra Leone.

Sweet potatoes are sometimes called yams. The word *yam* came from a West African language.

BEAUFORT'S GULLAH FESTIVAL

Shouts and drumbeats fill the air. Dancers in colorful African costumes whirl and sway. You're watching the Original Gullah Festival in Beaufort!

This festival celebrates the **culture** of the Gullah people. They live on South Carolina's Sea Islands. The Gullah are descended from enslaved West African people. They keep much of their culture alive. That includes their language, storytelling, music, and dances.

The Gullah people are also excellent basket weavers. Stop by to learn how they make them!

TOURING THE BMW FACTORY NEAR GREENVILLE

Some workers are **welding** metals. They wear masks to protect their faces. Others work at long lines of machinery. Finally, out come the finished products. Shiny new cars!

You're touring the BMW car plant. It's one of the state's many busy factories. Manufacturing grew after the Civil War. Many textile mills opened in the late 1800s. They turned raw cotton into cloth.

More new factories sprang up. By the mid-1950s, the state had changed. More people worked in factories than on farms!

Check out how these luxurious cars are made at the BMW car plant.

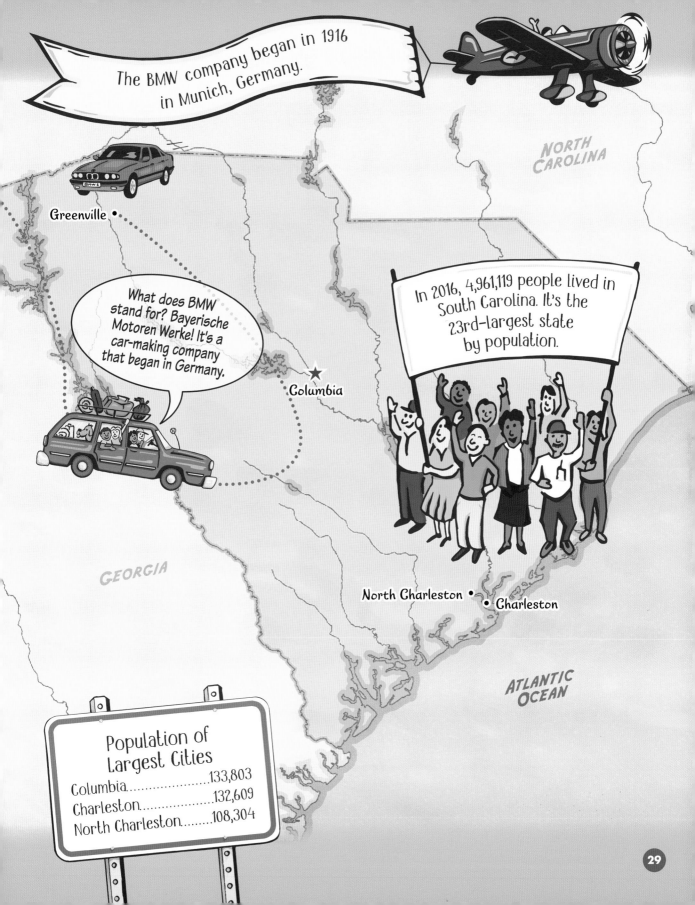

What's Made in South Carolina? Chemicals, textiles, and forest products

• Greenwood

GEORGIA

NORTH CAROLINA

Yum! Look at all the stuff they make with goat's milk. Cheese, yogurt, ice cream, and fudge!

In 1920, South Carolina had 167 textile mills. Approximately 50,000 people worked in the mills. They made cotton cloth.

Many South Carolina workers have service jobs. Some work in stores, hotels, schools, or hospitals. Others drive trucks, program computers, or repair bikes.

ATLANTIC OCEAN

What's Mined in South Carolina? Granite and limestone

EMERALD FARM IN GREENWOOD

Looking for a really unusual factory tour? This one is on a goat farm!

Emerald Farm in Greenwood raises goats. The farm has a soap factory. It makes soap out of goat's milk! You're welcome to visit the farm. You can pet the goats. Then watch how the soap is made.

South Carolina factories make much more than soap. The leading factory goods are chemicals. They include plastics and medicines. Textiles, or cloth, are important, too. Some factories make cotton, silk, or wool cloth. Others make polyester, rayon, or nylon. Paper and machines are some other factory goods.

Need a bar of soap? Look no further than the goats of Emerald Farm!

THE WORLD GRITS FESTIVAL IN SAINT GEORGE

First you get weighed. Then you plunge into a pool of grits. That's a mush of ground-up corn kernels. You **wallow** around for ten seconds. Then you get weighed again. You're hoping lots of grits stuck to you. Whoever gains the most weight is the winner!

You're in the Rolling in the Grits Contest. It's a fun event at the World Grits Festival in Saint George!

South Carolina has plenty of grits to eat. Corn is a big crop in the state. Tobacco is the top crop, though. Shrubs and flowers are important crops, too. Chickens bring in even more income than crops. Farmers also raise turkeys, cattle, and hogs.

Talk about playing with your food! Be sure to enter the Rolling in the Grits Contest!

Hampton and Pageland hold watermelon festivals every year.

Forget rolling in the grits. I want to enter the grits eating contest!

The state fair is held in Columbia in October each year.

The Lee County Cotton Festival is in Bishopville.

Golden Creek Mill in Easley is a restored 1815 mill with a waterwheel. It grinds cornmeal, grits, and flour.

Hominy is the best type of corn for making grits. Hominy is made from corn kernels with the hull removed. The kernels become plump when they're soaked or boiled.

What Does South Carolina Raise? Broilers (chickens), peaches, greenhouse and nursery products, and tobacco

• Easley

Pageland •

• Bishopville

Columbia

• Saint George

• Hampton

NORTH CAROLINA

GEORGIA

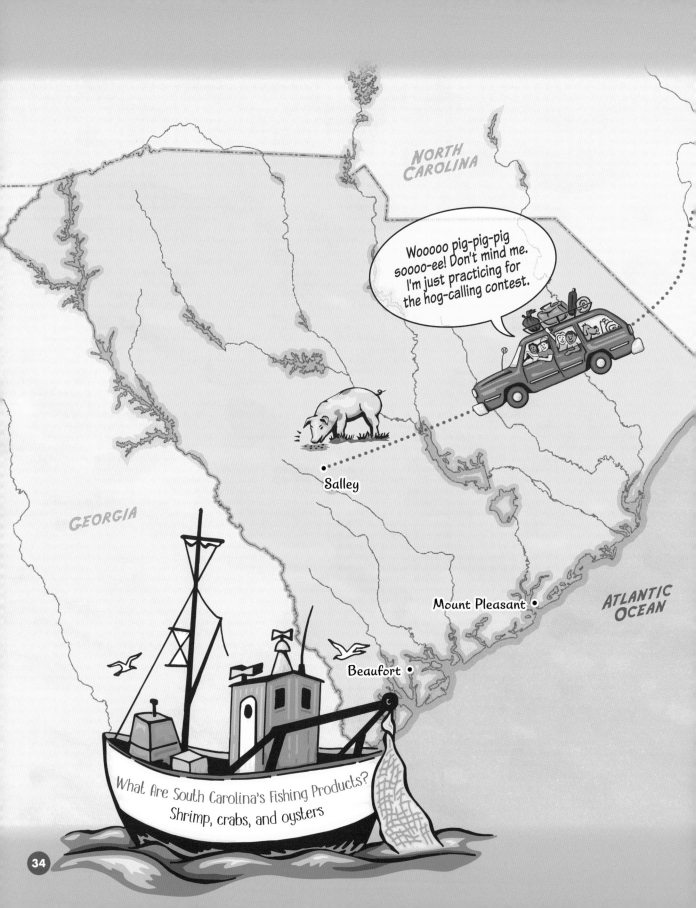

Put on your hog hat. You'll fit right in at the Chitlin Strut parade!

The Chitlin Strut is a big food festival. It takes place in the tiny town of Salley. Thousands of people show up every year. But what are chitlins?

Chitlins are a traditional southern food. The word *chitlins* is short for "chitterlings." They're hog intestines, boiled and deep-fried—yum!

South Carolina has lots of food festivals. Beaufort is known for its shrimp festival. Mount Pleasant holds a seafood festival every year. It also hosts the Lowcountry Oyster Festival. It's called the world's largest oyster festival!

Yum! First eat, then strut!

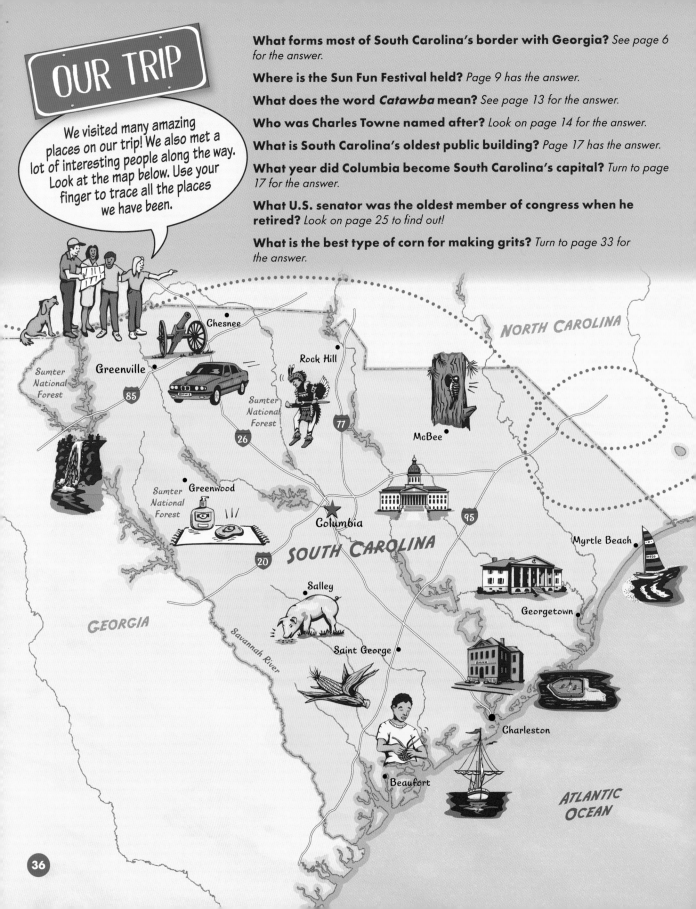

OUR TRIP

We visited many amazing places on our trip! We also met a lot of interesting people along the way. Look at the map below. Use your finger to trace all the places we have been.

What forms most of South Carolina's border with Georgia? *See page 6 for the answer.*

Where is the Sun Fun Festival held? *Page 9 has the answer.*

What does the word *Catawba* mean? *See page 13 for the answer.*

Who was Charles Towne named after? *Look on page 14 for the answer.*

What is South Carolina's oldest public building? *Page 17 has the answer.*

What year did Columbia become South Carolina's capital? *Turn to page 17 for the answer.*

What U.S. senator was the oldest member of congress when he retired? *Look on page 25 to find out!*

What is the best type of corn for making grits? *Turn to page 33 for the answer.*

NORTH CAROLINA

Chesnee

Rock Hill

Greenville

Sumter National Forest

85

Sumter National Forest

26

77

McBee

Greenwood

Sumter National Forest

95

Columbia

SOUTH CAROLINA

Myrtle Beach

20

Salley

GEORGIA

Savannah River

Saint George

Georgetown

Charleston

Beaufort

ATLANTIC OCEAN

STATE SYMBOLS

State animal: White-tailed deer

State beverage: Milk

State bird: Carolina wren

State botanical garden: Botanical Garden at Clemson University

State dance: Shag

State dog: Boykin spaniel

State fish: Striped bass

State flower: Yellow jessamine

State fruit: Peach

State gemstone: Amethyst

State insect: Carolina mantis (praying mantis)

State reptile: Loggerhead sea turtle

State shell: Lettered olive

State stone: Blue granite

State tree: Palmetto

State wild game bird: Wild turkey

STATE SONG

"CAROLINA"

Words by Henry Timrod, music by Anne Curtis Burgess

Call on thy children of the hill,
Wake swamp and river, coast and rill,
Rouse all thy strength and all thy skill,
Carolina! Carolina!

Hold up the glories of thy dead;
Say how thy elder children bled,
And point to Eutaw's battle-bed,
Carolina! Carolina!

Thy skirts indeed the foe may part,
Thy robe be pierced with sword and dart,

They shall not touch thy noble heart,
Carolina! Carolina!

Throw thy bold banner to the breeze!
Front with thy ranks the threatening seas
Like thine own proud armorial trees,
Carolina! Carolina!

Girt with such wills to do and bear,
Assured in right, and mailed in prayer,
Thou wilt not bow thee to despair,
Carolina! Carolina!

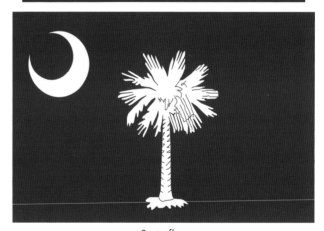

State flag

That was a great trip! We have traveled all over South Carolina! There are a few places that we didn't have time for, though. Next time, we plan to visit Ripley's Aquarium in Myrtle Beach. Visitors can see 10-foot (3-m) sharks and other amazing sea life. Scientists even conduct hourly dives and marine education classes!

State seal

FAMOUS PEOPLE

Anderson, Bill (1937–), country singer

Ansari, Aziz (1983–), comedian and actor

Baldwin, James Mark (1861–1934), psychologist

Baruch, Bernard (1870–1965), businessman and statesman

Bethune, Mary McLeod (1875–1955), educator

Brown, James (1933–2006), singer

Byars, Betsy (1928–), children's author

Calhoun, John C. (1782–1850), statesman

Davis, Viola (1965–), actress

Frazier, Joe (1944–2011), boxer

Gibson, Althea (1927–2003), tennis player

Gillespie, John Birks "Dizzy" (1917–1993), jazz musician

Heyward, DuBose (1885–1940), poet, author, playwright

Hunter-Gault, Charlayne (1942–), journalist

Jackson, Andrew (1767–1845), seventh U.S. president

Jackson, Jesse (1941–), civil rights leader

Jackson, "Shoeless" Joe (1888–1951), baseball player

Kitt, Eartha (1927–2008), singer, actor

McNair, Ronald (1950–1986), astronaut

Rock, Chris (1965–), comedian and actor

Rucker, Darius (1966–), singer and songwriter

Thurmond, Strom (1902–2003), senator

Townes, Charles H. (1915–2015), physicist

White, Vanna (1957–), TV performer

WORDS TO KNOW

colonists (KOL-uh-nists) people who settle a new land for their home country

colony (KOL-uh-nee) a land with ties to a mother country

culture (KUHL-chur) a group of people's customs and ways of life

mansion (MAN-shuhn) a large, elegant house

plantation (plan-TAY-shuhn) a large farm that raises mainly one crop

reservation (rez-ur-VAY-shuhn) land set aside for a special use, such as for Native Americans

swamps (SWAHMPS) wetlands

traditional (truh-DISH-uhn-ul) following long-held customs

wallow (WOL-oh) to roll around in something such as mud

welding (WELD-ing) joining metal parts by applying intense heat

TO LEARN MORE

IN THE LIBRARY

Cunningham, Kevin. *The South Carolina Colony.* New York, NY: Scholastic, 2011.

Felix, Rebecca. *What's Great About South Carolina?* Minneapolis, MN: Lerner Publishing Group, 2015.

Jerome, Kate Boehm. *South Carolina: What's so Great About This State?* Mount Pleasant, SC: Arcadia Kids, 2010.

ON THE WEB

Visit our Web site for links about South Carolina:

childsworld.com/links

Note to Parents, Teachers, and Librarians: We routinely verify our Web links to make sure they are safe and active sites. So encourage your readers to check them out!

PLACES TO VISIT OR CONTACT

The South Carolina Historical Society

schistory.org

100 Meeting Street

Charleston, SC 29401

843/723-3225

For more information about the history of South Carolina

South Carolina Tourism

discoversouthcarolina.com

1205 Pendleton Street

Columbia, SC 29201

803/734-0124

For more information about traveling in South Carolina

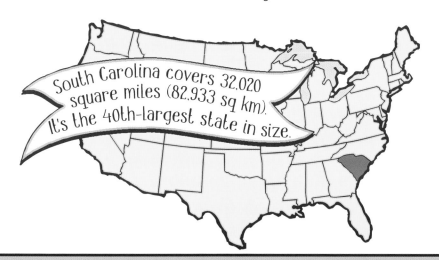

South Carolina covers 32,020 square miles (82,933 sq km). It's the 40th-largest state in size.

INDEX

Bye, Palmetto State.
We had a great time.
We'll come back soon!